EASY
Desserts

EASY
Desserts

LOVE FOOD

Love Food ® is an imprint of Parragon Books Ltd

Parragon
Queen Street House
4 Queen Street
Bath BA1 1HE, UK

Copyright © Parragon Books Ltd 2009

Love Food ® and the accompanying heart device is a trademark of Parragon Books Ltd

Cover and additional photography by Charlie Richards*
Additional food styling by Mary Wall
Introduction by Anne Sheasby

ISBN: 978-1-4075-2868-7

Printed in Indonesia

NOTES FOR THE READER
This book uses imperial, metric, and US cup measurements. Follow the same units of measurement throughout; do not mix imperial and metric. All spoon measurements are level: teaspoons are assumed to be 5 ml, and tablespoons are assumed to be 15 ml. Unless otherwise stated, milk is assumed to be full fat, eggs and individual fruits are medium
The times given are an approximate guide only. Preparation times differ according to the techniques used by different people and the cooking times may also vary from those given. Optional ingredients, variations or serving suggestions have not been included in the calculations.
Recipes using raw or very lightly cooked eggs should be avoided by infants, the elderly, pregnant women, convalescents, and anyone with an illness. Pregnant and breastfeeding women are advised to avoid eating peanuts and peanut products.
Vegetarians should be aware that some of the ready-prepared ingredients used in the recipes in this book may contain animal products. Always check the packaging before use.

*pages 10, 14, 19, 20, 29, 31, 37, 53, 54, 57, 60, 63, 65, 66, 69, 72, 77, 93, 95, 99, 101, 102, 105, 107, 108, 113, 117, 125, 127, 131, 133, 137, 139, 140 and 149.

Contents

Introduction

A delicious dessert provides the perfect finale to many meals and offers a tempting sweet treat that so many of us enjoy.

Desserts vary enormously and they don't have to be indulgent to be enjoyable. You may prefer to choose a rich and creamy concoction or a chocolate-laden creation, but on other occasions you may favor a lighter or more fruity combination. While a crème brulee, trifle, or another cream-based dessert will satisfy that craving for something sweet, a simple fruit salad or compote provides a light and refreshing end to a meal.

Desserts to Suit all Occasions

Many different desserts, both hot and cold, can be created from the wide range of ingredients that are readily available to us, thus providing the perfect conclusion to many meals. Make the most of fruits and other ingredients in season, when they are in prime condition and at their most abundant, to create some really scrumptious desserts.

Fruit desserts, pies, tarts, and pastries, sponges, creamy desserts and cheesecakes, mousses and gelatins, meringues, ices and iced desserts, and so on, provide plenty of choice to suit all occasions. Perhaps you are planning a dessert for a family meal, a mid-week supper for two, an informal get-together with friends, a buffet or a sophisticated dinner party, or maybe you are simply someone who wants to satisfy your sweet tooth.

Selecting Which Type of Dessert to Make

It is important to consider the rest of the meal when choosing a dessert and to pick a dessert that balances well with, and complements, the other dishes being served. The occasion, the number of people you are serving, the preparation time you have available, and the time of year are all important aspects to consider when selecting a dessert.

For example, presenting a hot dessert to guests on a scorching summer's day would not be the most popular choice. Instead, serve a cold, perhaps fruit-based, dessert, such as a chilled cheesecake, soufflé, or fruit mousse on a hot day, and save the old favorites, such as pies, crumbles, and other baked desserts, for cheering up those crisp fall or chilly winter days.

Other factors to consider include whether or not you decide to offer a choice and serve more than one dessert to your companions. Perhaps instead of presenting the dessert in one large serving dish, you may choose to make individual portions (these are especially good for dinner parties). Also bear in mind how easy the dessert will be to serve and if it can be cut into portions beforehand to make it easier to serve at the table. Think about whether the dessert can be prepared in advance or if it may need some last-minute attention—if so, how does this fit with the occasion and the time available?

Decorating Desserts

A simple decoration is often all that is needed to ensure a dessert is as pleasing to the eye as it is to the palate. Fresh fruits make an easy and attractive decoration for many desserts, especially fresh berries, such as strawberries (used whole, halved, or sliced into fan shapes) or raspberries, small sprigs of red or white currants, or a cluster of cherries.

A scattering of seeds or whole, sliced, or chopped toasted nuts provides a decorative touch, as well as adding texture, flavor, and color. A simple dusting of sifted confectioners' sugar or unsweetened cocoa can provide the perfect finish. Edible flowers (such as pansies, roses, and nasturtiums) or small sprigs or leaves of fresh herbs (such as mint or lemon balm) can transform a dessert.

Frosted fruits, such as grapes, small berries, or cherries (dipped in egg white and superfine sugar, then left to dry), frosted leaves or flowers, or chocolate-dipped fruits provide a lovely finishing touch. Citrus fruit slices or twists, or curls of thinly pared citrus zest create an effective, delicate decoration.

Last but by no means least, chocolate provides the perfect decoration for numerous desserts. Grated chocolate, chocolate curls, scrolls, ruffles, leaves, or lacy lattices, or a drizzle of melted chocolate will transform the simplest of desserts into something really impressive.

Serving Desserts

Many desserts are best served simply on their own, but some are made even more appealing when served with, for example, a homemade cookie, wafer, brandy snap, or amaretti, a scoop or two of ice cream or sherbet, a dollop of whipped cream, plain yogurt or crème fraiche, or a spoonful or two of hot custard. Simple sweet sauces, fruit coulis, or fruit purees also add that extra finishing touch to a variety of desserts.

1

Pies & Pastries

Apple Pie

serves 4

pie dough

scant 2½ cups all-purpose flour

pinch of salt

6 tbsp butter or margarine, cut into small pieces

6 tbsp lard or white vegetable fat, cut into small pieces

about 6 tbsp cold water

beaten egg or milk, for glazing

filling

1 lb 10 oz–2 lb 4 oz/ 750 g–1 kg cooking apples, peeled, cored, and sliced

⅔ cup light brown or superfine sugar, plus extra for sprinkling

½–1 tsp ground cinnamon, mixed spice, or ground ginger

1–2 tbsp water (optional)

To make the pie dough, sift the flour and salt into a mixing bowl. Add the butter and fat and rub it in with your fingertips until the mixture resembles fine breadcrumbs. Add the water and gather the mixture together into a dough. Wrap the dough in plastic wrap and chill in the refrigerator for 30 minutes.

Preheat the oven to 425°F/220°C. Roll out almost two thirds of the dough thinly and use to line a deep 9-inch/ 23-cm pie plate or pie pan.

Mix the apples with the sugar and spice and pack into the pastry shell; the filling can come up above the rim. Add the water if needed, particularly if the apples are not very juicy.

Roll out the remaining dough to form a lid. Dampen the edges of the pie rim with water and position the lid, pressing the edges firmly together. Trim and crimp the edges.

Use the trimmings to cut out leaves or other shapes to decorate the top of the pie, dampen, and attach. Glaze the top of the pie with beaten egg or milk, make 1–2 slits in the top, and place the pie on a baking sheet.

Bake in the preheated oven for 20 minutes, then reduce the temperature to 350°F/180°C and bake for an additional 30 minutes, or until the pastry is a light golden brown. Serve hot or cold, sprinkled with sugar.

Lemon Meringue Pie

serves 4

pie dough

scant 1½ cups all-purpose flour

7 tbsp butter, diced, plus extra for greasing

scant ½ cup confectioners' sugar

finely grated rind of 1 lemon

1 egg yolk, beaten

3 tbsp milk

filling

3 tbsp cornstarch

1¼ cups cold water

juice and grated rind of 2 lemons

heaping ¾ cup superfine sugar

2 eggs, separated

To make the dough, sift the flour into a large bowl and rub in the butter. Then mix in the remaining ingredients. Knead briefly on a lightly floured work surface. Let rest for 30 minutes.

Preheat the oven to 350°F/180°C. Grease an 8-inch/20-cm ovenproof tart pan with butter.

Roll out the dough to a thickness of ¼ inch/5 mm and line the pan with it. Prick with a fork, then line with parchment paper and fill with dried beans. Bake for 15 minutes. Remove from the oven, then reduce the oven temperature to 300°F/150°C.

To make the filling, mix the cornstarch with a little water to make a paste. Pour the remaining water into a saucepan. Stir in the lemon juice and rind and cornstarch paste. Bring to a boil, while stirring, and cook for 2 minutes. Cool slightly, then stir in 5 tablespoons of the sugar and the egg yolks and pour into the pastry shell. In a separate bowl, whisk the egg whites until stiff. Gradually whisk in the remaining sugar and spread over the pie.

Bake for 40 minutes, until the meringue is light brown, and serve warm.

Banoffee Toffee Pie

serves 4

28 fl oz/800 ml canned
sweetened condensed
milk

6 tbsp butter, melted, plus
extra for greasing

1¾ cups graham crackers,
crushed into crumbs

scant ½ cup almonds,
toasted and ground

scant ½ cup hazelnuts,
toasted and ground

4 ripe bananas

1 tbsp lemon juice

1 tsp vanilla extract

2¾ oz/75 g chocolate,
grated

2 cups heavy cream,
whipped

Place the cans of condensed milk in a large saucepan and cover them with water. Bring to a boil, then reduce the heat and simmer for 2 hours. Ensure the water is added to regularly to keep the cans covered. Carefully lift out the hot cans and let cool.

Preheat the oven to 350°F/180°C. Grease a 9-inch/23-cm loose-bottom tart pan with butter. Place the remaining butter in a bowl and add the crackers and nuts. Mix together well, then press the mixture evenly into the bottom and sides of the pan. Bake for 10–12 minutes, remove from the oven, and let cool.

Peel and slice the bananas and place them in a bowl. Sprinkle over the lemon juice and vanilla extract and mix gently. Spread the banana mixture over the cracker crust in the pan, then open the cans of condensed milk and spoon the contents over the bananas. Sprinkle over 1¾ oz/50 g of the chocolate, then top with a thick layer of whipped cream. Scatter over the remaining chocolate, transfer to a plate, and serve.

Mississippi Mud Pie

serves 4

pie dough

heaping 1¾ cups
all-purpose flour, plus
extra for dusting

2 tbsp unsweetened cocoa

½ cup plus 2 tbsp butter

2 tbsp superfine sugar

1–2 tbsp cold water

filling

¾ cup butter

scant 1¾ cups packed
brown sugar

4 eggs, lightly beaten

4 tbsp unsweetened cocoa,
sifted

5½ oz/150 g semisweet
chocolate

1¼ cups light cream

1 tsp chocolate extract

to garnish

scant 2 cups heavy cream,
whipped

chocolate flakes

chocolate curls

To make the dough, sift the flour and cocoa into a mixing bowl. Rub in the butter with your fingertips until the mixture resembles fine breadcrumbs. Stir in the sugar and enough cold water to mix to a soft dough. Wrap the dough and chill in the refrigerator for 15 minutes.

Preheat the oven to 375°F/190°C. Roll out the dough on a lightly floured work surface and use to line a 9-inch/23-cm loose-bottom tart pan. Line with parchment paper and fill with dried beans. Bake in the preheated oven for 15 minutes. Remove the paper and beans from the pastry shell and cook for another 10 minutes until crisp.

To make the filling, beat the butter and sugar together in a bowl and gradually beat in the eggs with the cocoa. Melt the chocolate and beat it into the mixture with the cream and the chocolate extract.

Reduce the oven temperature to 325°F/160°C. Pour the mixture into the pastry shell and bake for 45 minutes, or until the filling has set.

Let the mud pie cool completely, then transfer it to a serving plate, if you like. Cover with the whipped cream. Decorate the pie with chocolate flakes and chocolate curls, then chill until ready to serve.

Pumpkin Pie

serves 6

4 lb/1.8 kg sweet pumpkin

4 tbsp cold unsalted butter, cut into small pieces, plus extra for greasing

1 cup all-purpose flour, plus extra for dusting

1/4 tsp baking powder

1 1/2 tsp ground cinnamon

3/4 tsp ground nutmeg

3/4 tsp ground cloves

1 tsp salt

1/4 cup superfine sugar

3 eggs

1 3/4 cups sweetened condensed milk

1/2 tsp vanilla extract

1 tbsp raw sugar

streusel topping

2 tbsp all-purpose flour

4 tbsp raw sugar

1 tsp ground cinnamon

2 tbsp cold unsalted butter, cut into small pieces

heaping 2/3 cup shelled pecans, chopped

heaping 2/3 cup shelled walnuts, chopped

Preheat the oven to 375°F/190°C. Halve the pumpkin and remove the seeds, stem, and stringy insides. Discard the stem and stringy insides. Place the pumpkin halves, face down, in a shallow baking pan and cover with foil. Bake for 1 1/2 hours, then let cool.

Scoop out the flesh, and mash with a potato masher or puree it in a food processor. Drain away any excess liquid. Cover with plastic wrap and let chill until ready to use.

To make the pie dough, first grease a 9-inch/23-cm round pie plate with butter. Sift the flour and baking powder into a large bowl. Stir in 1/2 tsp cinnamon, 1/4 tsp nutmeg, 1/4 tsp cloves, 1/2 tsp salt, and all the superfine sugar. Rub in the butter with the fingertips until the mixture resembles fine breadcrumbs, then make a well in the center. Lightly beat 1 egg and pour it into the well. Mix together until a soft dough is formed. Roll out the pastry on a lightly floured surface and use to line the pie plate, trimming the edges. Cover and chill in the refrigerator for 30 minutes.

Preheat the oven to 425°F/220°C. To make the filling, stir the condensed milk and remaining eggs into the pumpkin puree. Add the remaining spices and salt, then stir in the vanilla extract and raw sugar. Pour into the pastry shell and bake for 15 minutes.

Meanwhile, make the topping. Combine the flour, sugar, and cinnamon in a bowl, rub in the butter until crumbly, then stir in the nuts. Remove the pie from the oven and reduce the heat to 350°F/180°C. Sprinkle the topping over the pie, then bake for an additional 35 minutes. Serve hot or cold.

Tarte au Citron

serves 4

pie dough

scant 1½ cups all-purpose flour, plus extra for dusting

3 tbsp ground almonds

7 tbsp butter, diced, plus extra for greasing

scant ½ cup confectioners' sugar, sifted

finely grated rind of 1 lemon

1 egg yolk, beaten

3 tbsp milk

filling

4 eggs

1¼ cups superfine sugar

juice and finely grated rind of 2 lemons

⅔ cup heavy cream

mascarpone cheese, to serve

To make the pie dough, sift the flour into a bowl. Mix in the almonds, then rub in the butter. Mix in the confectioners' sugar, lemon rind, egg yolk, and milk. Knead briefly on a lightly floured work surface, then let rest for 30 minutes.

Preheat the oven to 350°F/180°C. Grease a 9-inch/ 23-cm tart pan with butter. Roll out the dough to a thickness of ¼ inch/5 mm and use to line the bottom and sides of the pan. Prick all over with a fork, line with parchment paper, and fill with dried beans. Bake for 15 minutes.

Remove from the oven. Reduce the oven temperature to 300°F/150°C.

To make the filling, crack the eggs into a bowl. Whisk in the sugar, then the lemon juice and rind and cream. Spoon into the pastry shell and bake for 45 minutes. Remove from the oven and let cool for 45 minutes. Serve the tart topped with mascarpone cheese.

Paper-Thin Fruit Pies

makes 4

1 apple

1 ripe pear

2 tbsp lemon juice

½ cup butter

4 sheets filo dough, thawed if frozen

2 tbsp apricot jelly

1 tbsp orange juice

1 tbsp chopped pistachios

2 tsp confectioners' sugar, for dusting

Preheat the oven to 400°F/200°C. Core and thinly slice the apple and pear and immediately toss them in the lemon juice to prevent discoloration.

Melt the butter in a pan over low heat. Cut each sheet of dough into 4 and cover with a clean, damp dish towel. Brush a 4-cup nonstick muffin pan (cup size 4 inches/10 cm in diameter) with a little of the butter.

Working on each pie separately, brush 4 small sheets of dough with butter. Press a sheet of dough into the bottom of 1 cup. Arrange the other sheets of dough on top at slightly different angles. Repeat with the other sheets of dough to make another 3 pies.

Arrange the apple and pear slices alternately in the center of each pie shell and lightly crimp the edge of the dough of each pie.

Stir the jelly and orange juice together until smooth and brush over the fruit. Bake in the preheated oven for 12–15 minutes. Sprinkle with the pistachios, dust lightly with confectioners' sugar, and serve hot, straight from the oven.

Maple Pecan Pies

makes 12

filling

1 cup all-purpose flour, plus extra for dusting

6 tbsp butter, cut into small pieces

¼ cup superfine sugar

2 egg yolks

filling

2 tbsp maple syrup

⅔ cup heavy cream

½ cup superfine sugar

pinch of cream of tartar

6 tbsp water

1 cup shelled pecans, chopped

12–24 pecan halves, to decorate

Preheat the oven to 400°F/200°C. To make the pie dough, sift the flour into a mixing bowl and rub in the butter with your fingertips until the mixture resembles breadcrumbs. Add the sugar and egg yolks and mix to form a soft dough. Wrap the dough in plastic wrap and let chill in the refrigerator for 30 minutes.

On a lightly floured work sourface, roll out the pie dough thinly, cut out 12 circles, and use to line 12 tart pans. Prick the bottoms with a fork. Line with parchment paper and fill with dried beans. Bake in the oven for 10–15 minutes, or until light golden. Remove from the oven and take out the paper and beans. Bake the pastry shells for an additional 2–3 minutes. Let cool on a wire rack.

Mix half the maple syrup and half the cream in a bowl. Place the sugar, cream of tartar, and water in a pan and heat gently until the sugar dissolves. Bring to a boil and boil until light golden. Remove from the heat and stir in the maple syrup and cream mixture.

Return the pan to the heat and cook to the soft ball stage (240°F/116°C): that is, when a little of the mixture dropped into a bowl of cold water forms a soft ball. Stir in the remaining cream and let cool. Brush the remaining maple syrup over the edges of the pies. Place the chopped pecans in the pastry shells and spoon in the toffee. Top each pie with 1 or 2 pecan halves. Let cool completely before serving.

Chocolate Blueberry Pies

makes 10

pie dough

scant 1¼ cups all-purpose flour

½ cup unsweetened cocoa

¼ cup superfine sugar

pinch of salt

½ cup butter, cut into small pieces

1 egg yolk

1–2 tbsp cold water

sauce

1½ cups blueberries

2 tbsp crème de cassis

2 tbsp confectioners' sugar, sifted

filling

5 oz/140 g semisweet chocolate

1 cup heavy cream

⅔ cup sour cream

To make the pie dough, place the flour, cocoa, sugar, and salt in a large bowl and rub in the butter until the mixture resembles breadcrumbs. Add the egg and a little cold water to form a dough. Wrap the dough in plastic wrap and let chill in the refrigerator for 30 minutes.

Remove the pie dough from the refrigerator and roll out. Use to line ten 4-inch/10-cm tart pans. Freeze for 30 minutes. Preheat the oven to 350°F/180°C. Bake the pastry shells in the oven for 15–20 minutes. Let cool.

Place the blueberries, cassis, and confectioners' sugar in a pan and warm through so that the berries become shiny but do not burst. Let cool.

To make the filling, melt the chocolate in a heatproof bowl set over a pan of simmering water, then let cool slightly. Whip the cream until stiff and fold in the sour cream and melted chocolate.

Transfer the pastry shells to a serving plate and divide the chocolate filling among them, smoothing the surface with a spatula, then top with the blueberries.

Custard Tart

serves 8

pie dough

1 cup all-purpose flour,
plus extra for dusting

1–2 tbsp superfine sugar

heaping ½ cup butter, cut
into pieces

1 tbsp water

filling

3 eggs

⅔ cup light cream

⅔ cup milk

freshly grated nutmeg

whipping cream, to serve

To make the pie dough, place the flour and sugar in a large bowl and rub in the butter with your fingertips until the mixture resembles breadcrumbs.

Add the water and mix together to form a soft dough. Wrap in plastic wrap and let chill in the refrigerator for 30 minutes.

Roll out the dough on a lightly floured work surface to form a circle slightly larger than a 9½-inch/24-cm loose-bottom tart pan, then use to line the pan. Prick the dough with a fork and let chill for 30 minutes.

Preheat the oven to 375°F/190°C. Line the pastry shell with foil and dried beans and bake in the oven for 15 minutes. Remove the foil and beans and bake the pastry shell for an additional 15 minutes.

To make the filling, whisk the eggs, cream, milk, and nutmeg together. Pour the filling into the prepared pastry shell. Return the tart to the oven and cook for 25–30 minutes, or until just set. Serve with whipping cream, if you want.

Crème Brûlée Tarts

serves 6

pie dough

1¼ cups all-purpose flour, plus extra for dusting

2 tbsp superfine sugar

½ cup butter, diced

1 tbsp water

filling

4 egg yolks

¼ cup superfine sugar

1¾ cups heavy cream

1 tsp vanilla extract

raw brown sugar, for sprinkling

To make the dough, place the flour and sugar in a bowl and rub in the butter with your fingertips until the mixture resembles breadcrumbs. Add the water and bring the mixture together with your fingers to form a soft dough. Wrap in plastic wrap and chill in the refrigerator for 30 minutes.

Divide the dough into 6 pieces. Roll out the dough on a lightly floured work surface and use it to line 6 tartlet pans, 4 inches/10 cm wide. Prick the base of the dough with a fork and chill in the refrigerator for 20 minutes.

Line the tart shells with foil and dried beans and bake in a preheated oven, 375°F/190°C, for 15 minutes. Remove the foil and beans and cook for 10 minutes more, until crisp and golden. Let cool.

Meanwhile, make the filling. Beat the egg yolks and sugar together in a bowl until pale. Heat the cream and vanilla extract in a pan until just below boiling point, then pour onto the egg mixture, whisking continuously.

Return the mixture to a clean pan and bring to just below a boil, stirring continuously until thick. Do not let the mixture boil or it will curdle.

Let the mixture cool slightly, then pour into the tart shells. Let cool, then chill in the refrigerator overnight.

Sprinkle the tarts with brown sugar. Place under a preheated hot broiler for a few minutes. Let cool, then chill for 2 hours before serving.

Summer Fruit Tartlets

makes 12

pie dough

1⅓ cups all-purpose flour, plus extra for dusting

¾ cup confectioners' sugar

½ cup ground almonds

1 stick unsalted butter, diced and chilled

1 egg yolk

1 tbsp milk

filling

1½ cups cream cheese

confectioners' sugar, to taste, plus extra for dusting

12 oz/350 g fresh summer berries and currants, such as blueberries, raspberries, small strawberries, red currants, and white currants, picked over and prepared

To make the pie dough, sift the flour and sugar into a bowl, then stir in the almonds. Rub in the butter with your fingertips until the mixture resembles breadcrumbs. Add the egg yolk and milk and mix to form a dough. Turn out onto a lightly floured work surface in plastic wrap and knead briefly. Wrap and chill in the refrigerator for 30 minutes.

Preheat the oven to 400°F/200°C. Roll out the dough and use it to line 12 deep tart or individual brioche pans. Prick the pastry bottoms with a fork. Press a piece of foil into each tartlet, covering the edges, and bake in the preheated oven for 10–15 minutes, or until light golden brown. Remove the foil and bake for an additional 2–3 minutes. Transfer the pastry shells to a wire rack to cool.

To make the filling, mix the cream cheese and confectioners' sugar together in a bowl. Put a spoonful of filling in each pastry shell and arrange the fruit on top. Dust with sifted confectioners' sugar and serve immediately.

Truffled Honey Tart

serves 6

puff pastry

generous ¾ cup
all-purpose flour

pinch of salt

5 tbsp cold butter, cut into
pieces

1 tsp confectioners' sugar

cold water

filling

1⅛ cups curd cheese

scant ½ cup cream cheese

½ cup heavy cream

2 egg yolks, plus

1 whole egg

2 tbsp superfine sugar

4 tbsp flower honey, plus
extra for drizzling

crystallized violets or
sugared rose petals,
to decorate

Lightly grease a 9-inch/22-cm loose-bottom fluted tart pan. Sift the flour and salt into a food processor, add the butter, and process until the mixture resembles fine breadcrumbs. Turn the mixture into a large bowl, add the sugar, and a little cold water, just enough to bring the dough together. Turn out onto a work surface dusted with more flour and roll out the dough 3¼ inches/8 cm larger than the pan. Carefully lift the dough into the pan and press to fit. Roll the rolling pin over the pan to neaten the edges and trim the excess dough. Fit a piece of parchment paper into the tart shell, fill with dried beans, and let chill in the refrigerator for 30 minutes. Meanwhile, preheat the oven to 375°F/190°C.

Remove the pastry shell from the refrigerator and bake for 10 minutes in the preheated oven, then remove the beans and paper and bake for an additional 5 minutes.

To make the filling, mix the curd cheese, cream cheese, and cream together until smooth, then stir in the egg yolks, whole egg, sugar, and honey until completely smooth. Pour into the pastry shell and bake for 30 minutes. Remove from the oven and let cool in the pan for 10 minutes. Drizzle with more honey and decorate with violets.

Baklava

serves 4–6

1 cup shelled pistachios,
finely chopped

½ cup toasted hazelnuts,
finely chopped

½ cup blanched hazelnuts,
finely chopped

grated rind of 1 lemon

1 tbsp brown sugar

1 tsp ground allspice

scant ¾ cup butter, melted,
plus extra for greasing

9 oz/250 g (about 16 sheets)
frozen filo dough, thawed

1 cup water

2 tbsp clear honey

1 tbsp lemon juice

1½ cups superfine sugar

½ tsp ground cinnamon

Preheat the oven to 325°F/160°C. Place the nuts, lemon rind, sugar, and allspice in a bowl and mix well. Grease a round cake pan, 7 inches/18 cm in diameter and 2 inches/5 cm deep, with butter.

Cut the whole stack of filo sheets to the size of the pan. Keep the filo circles covered with a damp dish towel. Lay 1 circle on the bottom of the pan and brush with melted butter. Add another 6 circles on top, brushing between each layer with melted butter. Spread over one third of the nut mixture, then add 3 circles of buttered filo. Spread over another third of the nut mixture then top with 3 more circles of buttered filo. Spread over the remaining the nut mixture and add the last 3 circles of buttered filo. Cut into wedges, then bake in the oven for 1 hour.

Meanwhile, place the water, honey, lemon juice, superfine sugar, and cinnamon in a saucepan. Bring to a boil, stirring. Reduce the heat and simmer, without stirring, for 15 minutes. Cool.

Remove the baklava from the oven, pour over the syrup, and let set before serving.

Chocolate Filo Parcels

makes 18

2 oz/55 g semisweet chocolate, broken into pieces

¾ cup ground hazelnuts

1 tbsp finely chopped fresh mint

½ cup sour cream

2 apples

9 sheets filo dough, about 6 inches/15 cm square, thawed if frozen

4–6 tbsp butter, melted

confectioners' sugar, for dusting

Preheat the oven to 375°F/190°C. Break up the chocolate and melt in a heatproof bowl set over a saucepan of gently simmering water. Remove from the heat and let cool slightly.

Mix together the hazelnuts, mint, and sour cream in a bowl. Peel the apples and grate them into the bowl, then stir in the melted chocolate and mix well.

Cut each sheet of filo dough into 4 squares. Keep the squares you are not using covered with a damp dish towel. Brush 1 square with melted butter, place a second square on top, and brush with melted butter. Place a tablespoonful of the chocolate mixture in the center, then bring up the corners of the squares and twist together to enclose the filling completely. Continue making parcels in the same way until you have used up all the dough and filling.

Brush a cookie sheet with melted butter and place the parcels on it. Bake for about 10 minutes, until crisp and golden. Let cool slightly, then dust with confectioners' sugar and serve.

Pear & Pecan Strudel

serves 4

2 ripe pears

4 tbsp butter

1 cup fresh white breadcrumbs

⅓ cup shelled pecans, chopped

⅛ cup light brown sugar

finely grated rind of 1 orange

3½ oz/100 g filo dough, thawed if frozen

6 tbsp orange blossom honey

2 tbsp orange juice

confectioners' sugar, for dusting

Greek-Style yogurt, to serve (optional)

Preheat the oven to 400°F/200°C.

Peel, core, and chop the pears. Melt 1 tablespoon of the butter in a skillet and gently sauté the breadcrumbs until golden. Transfer the breadcrumbs to a bowl and add the pears, nuts, sugar, and orange rind. Place the remaining butter in a small saucepan and heat until melted.

Set aside 1 sheet of filo dough, keeping it well wrapped, and brush the remaining filo with a little melted butter. Spoon a little of the nut filling onto the first filo sheet, leaving a 1-inch/2.5-cm margin around the edge. Build up the strudel by placing buttered filo sheets on top of the first, spreading each one with nut filling as you build up the layers. Drizzle the honey and orange juice over the top.

Fold the short ends over the filling, then roll up, starting at a long side. Carefully lift onto a baking sheet, with the seam on top. Brush with any remaining melted butter and crumple the reserved sheet of filo pastry around the strudel. Bake for 25 minutes, or until golden and crisp. Dust with confectioners' sugar and serve warm with yogurt, if using.

Chocolate Nut Strudel

serves 6

¾ cup butter, plus extra for greasing

heaping 1¼ cups mixed chopped nuts

4 oz/115 g semisweet chocolate, chopped

4 oz/115 g milk chocolate, chopped

4 oz/115 g white chocolate, chopped

7 oz/200 g filo dough, thawed if frozen

3 tbsp corn syrup

½ cup confectioners' sugar

Preheat the oven to 375°F/190°C. Lightly grease a baking sheet with butter. Set aside 1 tablespoon of the nuts. Place the remaining nuts in a bowl and mix together with the 3 types of chocolate.

Place 1 sheet of filo dough on a clean dish towel. Melt the butter and brush the sheet of filo with the butter, drizzle with a little syrup, and sprinkle with some nuts and chocolate. Place another sheet of filo on top and repeat until you have used all the nuts and chocolate.

Use the dish towel to help you carefully roll up the strudel and place on the baking sheet, drizzle with a little more syrup, and sprinkle with the reserved nuts.

Bake in the preheated oven for 20–25 minutes. If the nuts start to brown too much, cover the strudel with a sheet of foil. Sprinkle the strudel with confectioners' sugar, slice, and serve warm.

Chocolate Éclairs

makes 12

choux pastry

5 tbsp butter, cut into small pieces, plus extra for greasing

⅔ cup water

¾ cup all-purpose flour, sifted

2 eggs

pastry cream

2 eggs, beaten lightly

¼ cup superfine sugar

2 tbsp cornstarch

1¼ cups milk

¼ tsp vanilla extract

frosting

2 tbsp butter

1 tbsp milk

1 tbsp unsweetened cocoa

½ cup confectioners' sugar

1¾ oz/50 g white chocolate, broken into pieces

Preheat the oven to 400°F/200°C.

Lightly grease a cookie sheet. Place the water in a saucepan, add the butter, and heat gently until the butter melts. Bring to a rolling boil, then remove the pan from the heat and add the flour all at once, beating well until the mixture leaves the sides of the pan and forms a ball. Let cool slightly, then gradually beat in the eggs to form a smooth, glossy mixture. Spoon into a large pastry bag fitted with a ½-inch/1-cm plain tip.

Sprinkle the cookie sheet with a little water. Pipe éclairs 3 inches/7.5 cm long, spaced well apart. Bake for 30–35 minutes, or until crisp and golden. Make a small slit in the side of each éclair to let the steam escape. Let cool on a wire rack.

Meanwhile, make the pastry cream. Whisk the eggs and sugar until thick and creamy, then fold in the cornstarch. Heat the milk until almost boiling and pour onto the eggs, whisking. Transfer to the saucepan and cook over low heat, stirring until thick. Remove the pan from the heat and stir in the vanilla extract. Cover with parchment paper and let cool.

To make the frosting, melt the butter with the milk in a saucepan, remove from the heat, and stir in the unsweetened cocoa and sugar. Split the éclairs lengthwise and pipe in the pastry cream. Spread the frosting over the top of the éclair. Melt a little white chocolate in a heatproof bowl set over a saucepan of gently simmering water, then spoon over the chocolate frosting, swirl in, and let set.

Profiteroles

serves 4
choux pastry

5 tbsp butter, plus extra for greasing

scant 1 cup cold water

¾ cup all-purpose flour

3 eggs, beaten

cream filling

1¼ cups heavy cream

3 tbsp superfine sugar

1 tsp vanilla extract

chocolate & brandy sauce

4½ oz/125 g semisweet chocolate, broken into pieces

2½ tbsp butter

6 tbsp water

2 tbsp brandy

Preheat the oven to 400°F/200°C and grease a large baking sheet with butter.

To make the pastry, place the water and butter in a saucepan and bring to a boil. Meanwhile, sift the flour into a bowl. Remove the pan from the heat and beat in the flour until smooth. Cool for 5 minutes. Beat in enough of the eggs to give the mixture a soft, dropping consistency. Transfer to a piping bag with a ½-inch/1-cm plain nozzle attached. Pipe small balls onto the baking sheet. Bake for 25 minutes. When removed from the oven, pierce each ball with a skewer in order to let steam escape.

To make the filling, whip together the cream, sugar, and vanilla extract. Cut the pastry balls almost in half, then fill with the cream.

To make the sauce, gently melt the chocolate and butter with the water in a small saucepan, stirring, until smooth. Stir in the brandy. Pile the profiteroles into individual serving dishes or into a pyramid on a raised cake stand. Pour over the sauce and serve.

Cakes & Bakes

Black Forest Gâteau

serves 8

3 tbsp butter, melted, plus extra for greasing

2 lb/900 g fresh cherries, pitted and halved

1¼ cups superfine sugar

⅓ cup cherry brandy

¾ cup all-purpose flour

½ cup unsweetened cocoa

½ tsp baking powder

4 eggs

4 cups heavy cream

grated semisweet chocolate and whole fresh cherries, to decorate

Preheat the oven to 350°F/180°C. Grease and line a 9-inch/23-cm springform cake pan.

Place the cherries in a saucepan and add 3 tablespoons of the sugar and the cherry brandy. Simmer for 5 minutes. Drain, reserving the syrup. In another bowl, sift together the flour, cocoa, and baking powder.

Place the eggs in a heatproof bowl and beat in ¾ cup of the sugar. Place the bowl over a saucepan of simmering water and beat for 6 minutes, or until thickened. Remove from the heat, then gradually fold in the flour mixture and melted butter. Spoon into the cake pan and bake for 40 minutes, then let cool.

Turn out the cake and cut in half horizontally. Mix the cream and the remaining sugar together and whip lightly. Spread the reserved syrup over the cut sides of the cake, then top with a layer of cream on each side. Arrange the cherries over one half of the cake, then place the other half on top of it. Cover the whole cake with cream, press grated chocolate all over the surface, and decorate with whole fresh cherries.

Mocha Layer Cake

serves 8

butter, for greasing

scant 2 cups self-rising
flour

¼ tsp baking powder

4 tbsp unsweetened cocoa

heaping ½ cup superfine
sugar

2 eggs

2 tbsp corn syrup

⅔ cup sunflower oil

⅔ cup milk

filling and topping

1 tsp instant coffee
granules

1 tbsp boiling water

1¼ cups heavy cream

2 tbsp confectioners' sugar

to decorate

1¾ oz/50 g chocolate
shavings

prepared chocolate caraque

confectioners' sugar,
for dusting

Preheat the oven to 350°F/180°C. Lightly grease three 7-inch/18-cm shallow cake pans.

Sift the flour, baking powder, and cocoa together into a large bowl. Stir in the superfine sugar, then make a well in the center. Add the eggs, syrup, oil, and milk to the well and gradually beat in with a wooden spoon to form a smooth batter. Divide among the prepared pans.

Bake in the preheated oven for 35–45 minutes, or until springy to the touch. Let cool slightly in the pans, then transfer to a wire rack and let cool completely.

To make the filling, dissolve the coffee in the boiling water and put in a bowl with the cream and confectioners' sugar. Whip until the cream is just holding its shape. Use half the cream to sandwich the 3 cakes together. Spread the remaining cream over the top and side of the cake.

To decorate, lightly press the chocolate shavings into the cream around the side of the cake.

Transfer to a serving plate. Lay the chocolate caraque over the top of the cake. Cut a few thin strips of parchment paper and arrange on top of the caraque. Dust with confectioners' sugar, then remove the paper.

Sachertorte

serves 10

heaping ½ cup butter, preferably unsalted, plus extra for greasing

6 oz/175 g semisweet chocolate, broken into pieces

scant ¾ cup superfine sugar

6 eggs, separated

scant 1¼ cups all-purpose flour

frosting and filling

8 oz/225 g semisweet chocolate, broken into pieces

5 tbsp cold strong black coffee

1 cup confectioners' sugar, sifted

6 tbsp good-quality apricot jelly, warmed

Preheat the oven to 300°F/150°C. Grease and line the bottom of a 9-inch/23-cm round springform cake pan. Melt the chocolate in a heatproof bowl set over a saucepan of barely simmering water. Cream the butter with a heaping ⅓ cup of the superfine sugar in a bowl until pale and fluffy. Add the egg yolks and beat well. Add the melted chocolate in a thin stream, beating well. Sift the flour, then fold into the mixture. Whisk the egg whites in a separate large, clean bowl until soft peaks form. Add the remaining superfine sugar and whisk until stiff and glossy. Fold half into the chocolate mixture, then fold in the remainder.

Spoon into the prepared pan and smooth the surface. Bake in the preheated oven for 1–1¼ hours, or until a skewer inserted into the center comes out clean. Let the cake cool slightly in the pan, then transfer to a wire rack and let cool completely.

To make the frosting, melt 6 oz/175 g of the chocolate in a heatproof bowl set over a saucepan of barely simmering water. Beat in the coffee. Whisk into the confectioners' sugar in a bowl to form a thick frosting. Cut the cake horizontally in half. Sandwich the layers together with the jelly. Invert the cake onto a wire rack. Spoon over the frosting and spread to coat the top and side. Let set for 5 minutes, letting any excess drip through the rack. Transfer to a serving plate and let set for at least 2 hours. Melt the remaining chocolate and spoon into a pastry bag fitted with a fine plain tip. Pipe "Sachertorte" on the cake top and let set.

White Truffle Cake

serves 12

butter, for greasing

1¾ oz/50 g white chocolate

2 eggs

¼ cup superfine sugar

½ cup all-purpose flour

truffle topping

1¼ cups heavy cream

12 oz/350 g white chocolate, broken into pieces

heaping 1 cup mascarpone cheese

to decorate

prepared chocolate caraque

unsweetened cocoa, for dusting

Preheat the oven to 350°F/180°C. Grease and line the bottom of an 8-inch/20-cm round springform cake pan. Melt the white chocolate in a heatproof bowl set over a saucepan of barely simmering water.

Using an electric mixer, beat the eggs and sugar together in a large bowl until thick and pale—the mixture should leave a trail when the whisk is lifted. Sift the flour and gently fold into the eggs with a metal spoon or palette knife. Add the melted chocolate. Pour the batter into the prepared pan and bake in the preheated oven for 25 minutes, or until springy to the touch. Let cool slightly in the pan, then transfer to a wire rack and let cool completely. Return the cold cake to the pan.

To make the topping, put the cream in a saucepan and bring to a boil, stirring continuously. Let cool slightly, then add the white chocolate and stir until melted and combined. Remove from the heat and set aside until almost cool, stirring, then mix in the mascarpone cheese. Pour on top of the cake. Let chill in the refrigerator for 2 hours.

To decorate, pick up the caraque carefully and arrange on the top of the cake, before dusting with cocoa.

Chocolate Fudge Gâteau

serves 10

1 tsp sunflower oil,
for oiling

3 oz/85 g semisweet
chocolate

1 cup butter, softened

scant 1¼ cups brown sugar

4 eggs, beaten

heaping 1½ cups
self-rising flour

heaping ½ cup ground
almonds

1–2 tbsp cooled, boiled water

4 oz/115 g soft vanilla
fudge, diced

2 oz/55 g grated
semisweet chocolate and
cocoa-dusted truffles,
to decorate

frosting

¾ cup butter, softened

2½ cups confectioners'
sugar, sifted

3–4 tbsp light cream

heaping ¼ cup light brown
sugar

1 tbsp unsweetened cocoa,
sifted

Preheat the oven to 350°F/180°C. Lightly oil and line the bottom of two 8-inch/20-cm shallow cake pans with parchment paper. Melt the chocolate in a heatproof bowl set over a saucepan of barely simmering water. Cream the butter and brown sugar together in a bowl until light and fluffy, then gradually add the eggs, beating well and adding a little of the flour after each addition. Gently fold in the melted chocolate and then the remaining flour until combined. Stir in the ground almonds with the water. Mix to form a soft dropping consistency. Stir in the fudge pieces, then divide among the prepared cake pans and smooth the surfaces.

Bake in the preheated oven for 35–40 minutes, or until springy to the touch. Let the cakes cool slightly in the pans, then transfer to a wire rack and let cool completely.

To make the frosting, beat the butter in a bowl until soft and creamy, then gradually beat in the confectioners' sugar, adding a little of the cream as the mixture becomes stiff. Add the brown sugar with the cocoa and gently stir. Stir in sufficient of the remaining cream to give a soft, spreadable frosting. Put the grated chocolate on a sheet of parchment paper. Cut the cakes horizontally in half and sandwich together with one third of the frosting. Spread another third around the side, then roll the cake in the grated chocolate. Transfer to a serving plate. Spread the top with the remaining frosting, piping rosettes around the outside edge for an attractive finish. Decorate with the truffles before serving.

Devil's Food Cake

serves 6

1 cup butter, plus extra for greasing

3½ oz/100 g semisweet chocolate, broken into pieces

scant 1⅓ cups self-rising flour

1 tsp baking soda

2½ cups light brown sugar

1 tsp vanilla extract

3 eggs

½ cup buttermilk

scant 1 cup boiling water

candied orange rind, to decorate

frosting

scant 1¼ cups superfine sugar

2 egg whites

1 tbsp lemon juice

3 tbsp orange juice

Preheat the oven to 375°F/190°C. Grease and line the bottom of two 8-inch/20-cm shallow cake pans. Melt the chocolate in a heatproof bowl set over a saucepan of barely simmering water. Sift the flour and baking soda together into a bowl.

Cream the butter and sugar together in a separate bowl until pale and fluffy. Beat in the vanilla extract and the eggs, one at a time, beating well after each addition. Add a little flour if the mixture starts to curdle.

Fold the melted chocolate into the mixture until well blended. Gradually fold in the remaining flour, then stir in the buttermilk and boiling water.

Divide the batter among the prepared pans and smooth the surfaces. Bake in the preheated oven for 30 minutes, or until springy to the touch. Let the cakes cool slightly in the pans, then transfer to a wire rack and let cool completely.

To make the frosting, put all the ingredients in a large heatproof bowl set over a saucepan of gently simmering water. Using an electric mixer, beat until thick and soft peaks form. Remove from the heat and beat until cool.

Sandwich the cakes together with some of the frosting. Swirl the remainder over the top and side of the cake. Decorate with candied orange rind.

Raspberry Dessert Cake

serves 9–10

heaping 1 cup bittersweet chocolate, broken into pieces

1 cup unsalted butter, plus extra for oiling

1 tbsp strong, dark coffee

5 eggs

heaping ½ cup golden superfine sugar

scant ⅔ cup all-purpose flour

1 tsp ground cinnamon

1 cup fresh raspberries, plus extra to serve

confectioners' sugar, for dusting

whipped cream, to serve

Preheat the oven to 325°F/160°C. Grease a 9-inch/23-cm cake pan and line the bottom with parchment paper. Put the chocolate, butter, and coffee in a small, heatproof bowl, set the bowl over a pan of barely simmering water, and heat until melted. Remove from the heat, stir, and let cool slightly.

Beat the eggs and superfine sugar together in a separate bowl until pale and thick. Gently fold in the chocolate mixture.

Sift the flour and cinnamon into another bowl, then fold into the chocolate mixture. Pour into the prepared pan and sprinkle the raspberries evenly over the top.

Bake in the preheated oven for about 35–45 minutes, or until the cake is well risen and springy to the touch. Let cool in the pan for 15 minutes before turning out onto a large serving plate. Dust with confectioners' sugar before serving with extra fresh raspberries and whipped cream.

Strawberry Cheesecake

serves 8

base

4 tbsp butter, preferably unsalted

2⅓ cups crushed graham crackers

½ cup chopped walnuts

filling

2 cups mascarpone cheese

2 eggs, beaten

3 tbsp superfine sugar

9 oz/250 g white chocolate, broken into pieces

10½ oz/300 g strawberries, hulled and quartered

topping

¾ cup mascarpone cheese

prepared chocolate caraque

16 whole strawberries

Preheat the oven to 300°F/150°C. Melt the butter in a saucepan over low heat and stir in the crushed crackers and the nuts. Spoon into a 9-inch/23-cm round springform cake pan and press evenly over the bottom with the back of a spoon. Set aside.

To make the filling, beat the mascarpone cheese in a bowl until smooth, then beat in the eggs and sugar. Melt the white chocolate in a heatproof bowl set over a saucepan of barely simmering water, stirring until smooth. Remove from the heat and let cool slightly, then stir into the cheese mixture. Stir in the strawberries.

Spoon the mixture into the cake pan, spread out evenly, and smooth the surface. Bake in the preheated oven for 1 hour, or until the filling is just firm. Turn off the oven and let the cheesecake cool inside with the door slightly ajar until completely cold. Transfer to a serving plate.

For the topping, spread the mascarpone cheese on top. Decorate with the chocolate caraque and whole strawberries.

Chocolate Panforte

serves 4–6

½ cup chopped candied orange peel

8 dried apricots, chopped

2 tbsp orange-flavored liqueur, such as Cointreau

1 cup shelled whole hazelnuts

heaping 1 cup sliced almonds, toasted

scant 1 cup all-purpose flour

2 tbsp unsweetened cocoa

2 tsp allspice

scant ¾ cup superfine sugar

5 tbsp clear honey

confectioners' sugar, to decorate

Preheat the oven to 300°F/150°C. Line an 8-inch/20-cm round cake pan. Put the orange peel, apricots, and liqueur into a heatproof bowl and let soak.

Toast the hazelnuts under a preheated medium broiler until the skins split, remove to a clean dish towel, and rub to remove the skins. Coarsely chop, then add to the fruit with the almonds and mix well.

Sift the flour, cocoa powder, and allspice into a separate bowl, then mix into the fruit and nuts. Bring the sugar and honey to a boil in a saucepan over low heat, stirring. Continue to boil, stirring, for 5 minutes, then quickly pour the syrup over the fruit and mix well. Turn into the prepared pan and level the surface. Bake in the oven for 50 minutes.

Remove from the oven, turn out on to a wire rack, and discard the lining paper. Let cool, then dredge with confectioners' sugar. Serve immediately, or store for up to 3–4 months in an airtight container.

Hot Chocolate Soufflé with Coffee Sabayon

serves 4–6

butter, for greasing

heaping ¼ cup golden superfine sugar, plus extra for coating

3 tbsp cornstarch

generous 1 cup milk

4 oz/115 g semisweet chocolate, broken into pieces

4 eggs, separated

confectioners' sugar, for dusting

sabayon

2 eggs

3 egg yolks

6 tbsp golden superfine sugar

4 tsp instant coffee granules

2 tbsp brandy

Preheat the oven to 375°F/190°C. Grease a 1-quart/1-liter soufflé dish with butter and coat with superfine sugar. To make the soufflé, place the cornstarch in a bowl. Add a little milk and stir until smooth. Pour the remaining milk into a heavy-bottom saucepan and add the chocolate. Heat gently until the chocolate has melted, then stir. Pour the chocolate milk onto the cornstarch paste, stirring. Return to the pan and bring to a boil, stirring. Let simmer for 1 minute. Remove from the heat and stir in the egg yolks, one at a time. Cover and let cool slightly.

Place the egg whites in a large, spotlessly clean, grease-free bowl and whisk until starting to stand in soft peaks. Gradually whisk in the superfine sugar until stiff but not dry. Stir a little of the meringue into the chocolate mixture, then carefully fold in the remainder. Pour into the prepared soufflé dish and bake in the preheated oven for 40 minutes, or until it is well risen and wobbles slightly when pushed.

Just before the soufflé is ready, make the coffee sabayon. Place all the ingredients in a heavy-bottom saucepan. Place the pan over very low heat and whisk constantly, until the mixture is thick and light. Dust a little confectioners' sugar over the soufflé and serve immediately, with the sabayon.

Rich Ginger Brownies with Port Cream

makes 8

7 oz/200 g semisweet chocolate

¾ cup unsalted butter

1 cup sugar

4 eggs, beaten

2 tsp vanilla extract

2 oz/55 g preserved ginger in syrup, chopped, plus 1 tbsp of the syrup

¾ cup all-purpose flour

2 tbsp chopped candied ginger, to decorate

port cream

scant 1 cup ruby port

scant 1 cup heavy cream

1 tbsp confectioners' sugar

1 tsp vanilla extract

Preheat the oven to 350°F/180°C. Grease a 9-inch/23-cm shallow, square cake pan.

Place the chocolate and butter in a saucepan and heat gently, stirring, until melted. Remove from the heat and stir in the sugar.

Beat the eggs, vanilla extract, and ginger syrup into the chocolate mixture. Stir in the flour and chopped ginger, mixing evenly.

Pour the mixture into the prepared pan and bake for 30–35 minutes, until just firm to the touch.

Meanwhile, make the port cream sauce. Place the port in a saucepan and simmer over medium–high heat until reduced to about 4 tablespoons. Remove from the heat and let cool. Whip the cream until beginning to thicken, then beat in the sugar, reduced port, and vanilla, continuing to whip until it holds soft peaks.

Remove the brownies from the oven, let cool for 2–3 minutes in the pan, then cut into 8 triangles. Place on individual serving plates and add a spoonful of port cream to each. Top with pieces of candied ginger and serve warm.

Individual Chocolate Desserts

serves 4

½ cup superfine sugar

3 eggs

½ cup all-purpose flour

½ cup unsweetened cocoa

scant ½ cup unsalted butter, melted, plus extra for greasing

3½ oz/100 g semisweet chocolate, melted

chocolate sauce

2 tbsp unsalted butter

3½ oz/100 g semisweet chocolate

5 tbsp water

1 tbsp superfine sugar

1 tbsp coffee-flavored liqueur, such as Kahlua

coffee beans, to decorate

To make the desserts, put the sugar and eggs into a heatproof bowl and place over a saucepan of simmering water. Whisk for about 10 minutes, until frothy. Remove the bowl from the heat and fold in the flour and cocoa. Fold in the butter, then the chocolate. Mix well.

Grease 4 small heatproof bowls with butter. Spoon the mixture into the bowls and cover with wax paper. Top with foil and secure with string. Place the desserts in a large saucepan filled with enough simmering water to reach halfway up the sides of the bowls. Steam for about 40 minutes, or until cooked through.

About 2–3 minutes before the end of the cooking time, make the sauce. Put the butter, chocolate, water, and sugar into a small saucepan and warm over low heat, stirring continuously, until melted together. Stir in the liqueur.

Remove the desserts from the heat, turn out into serving dishes, and pour over the sauce. Decorate with coffee beans and serve.

Toffee Sponge Cake

serves 4

½ cup golden raisins

¼ cup pitted dates, chopped

1 tsp baking soda

2 tbsp butter, plus extra for greasing

1 cup brown sugar

2 eggs

scant 1½ cups self-raising flour, sifted

sticky toffee sauce

2 tbsp butter

¾ cup heavy cream

1 cup brown sugar

zested orange rind, to decorate

freshly whipped cream, to serve

Put the fruits and baking soda into a heatproof bowl. Cover with boiling water and let soak.

Preheat the oven to 350°F/180°C. Grease an 8-inch/20-cm round cake pan with butter.

Put the remaining butter in a separate bowl, add the sugar, and mix well. Beat in the eggs then fold in the flour. Drain the soaked fruits, add to the bowl, and mix. Spoon the mixture evenly into the prepared cake pan. Transfer to the preheated oven and bake for 35–40 minutes. The cake is cooked when a skewer inserted into the center comes out clean.

About 5 minutes before the end of the cooking time, make the sauce. Melt the butter in a saucepan over medium heat. Stir in the cream and sugar and bring to a boil, stirring continuously. Reduce the heat and simmer for 5 minutes.

Turn out the cake onto a serving plate and pour over the sauce. Decorate with zested orange rind and serve with whipped cream.

Steamed Syrup Sponge Pudding

serves 4

butter, for greasing

2 tbsp dark corn syrup, plus extra to serve

½ cup butter

heaping ½ cup superfine sugar

2 eggs, lightly beaten

1¼ cups self-raising flour

2 tbsp milk

grated rind of 1 lemon

Butter two 1-pint/600-ml pudding basins and put equal amounts of the syrup into the bottoms.

Beat together the butter and sugar until soft and creamy, then beat in the eggs, a little at a time.

Fold in the flour and stir in the milk to make a soft dropping consistency. Add the lemon rind. Turn equal amounts of the mixture into the pudding basins.

Cover the surfaces with circles of parchment paper and top with a pleated sheet of foil. Secure with some string or crimp the edges of the foil to ensure a tight fit around the basins.

Place the puddings in a large saucepan half-filled with boiling water. Cover the saucepan and bring back to a boil over medium heat. Reduce the heat to a slow simmer and steam for 1½ hours until risen and firm. Keep checking the water level and top up with boiling water as necessary.

Remove the pan from the heat and lift out the pudding basins. Remove the covers and loosen the puddings from the sides of the basins using a knife.

Turn out into a warmed dish and heat a little more syrup to serve with the puddings.

Baked Rice

serves 4–6

1 tbsp melted butter

⅔ cup short-grain rice

heaping ⅓ cup superfine sugar

3½ cups milk

½ tsp vanilla extract

3 tbsp unsalted butter

whole nutmeg, for grating

cream, jelly, fruit puree, stewed fruit, or ice cream, to serve

Preheat the oven to 300°F/150°C. Grease a 1-quart/1.2-liter baking dish (a gratin dish is good) with the melted butter, place the rice in the dish, and sprinkle with the sugar.

Heat the milk in a saucepan until almost boiling, then pour over the rice. Add the vanilla extract and stir well to dissolve the sugar.

Cut the butter into small pieces and scatter over the surface of the rice.

Grate the whole nutmeg over the top, using as much as you like to give a good covering.

Place the dish on a baking sheet and bake in the center of the oven for 1½–2 hours, until well browned on the top. You can stir it after the first half hour to disperse the rice.

Serve hot with some cream, jelly, fresh fruit puree, stewed fruit, or ice cream. It is also good cold with fresh fruit, honey, or ice cream.

Ginger Baked Alaskas

serves 4

4 tbsp golden raisins or raisins

3 tbsp dark rum or ginger wine

4 square slices ginger cake

4 scoops vanilla ice cream or rum and raisin ice cream

3 egg whites

scant 1 cup granulated or superfine sugar

Preheat the oven to 450°F/230°C. Mix the golden raisins with the rum in a small bowl.

Place the cake slices well apart on a baking sheet and scatter a spoonful of the soaked golden raisins on each slice.

Place a scoop of ice cream in the center of each slice and place in the freezer.

Meanwhile, whisk the egg whites in a large grease-free bowl until soft peaks form, then gradually whisk the sugar into the egg whites, a tablespoonful at a time, until the mixture forms stiff peaks.

Remove the ice cream-topped cake slices from the freezer and spoon the meringue mixture over the ice cream. Spread to cover the ice cream completely.

Bake in the oven for about 5 minutes, until starting to brown. Serve immediately.

Meringue with Jelly Crumble

serves 4–6

2 tbsp butter

2½ cups milk

2 cups fresh white breadcrumbs

heaping ½ cup superfine sugar

grated rind of 1 lemon

3 eggs, separated

3 tbsp raspberry jelly, warmed

1 tsp golden granulated sugar

Preheat the oven to 350°F/180°C.

Using a little of the butter, grease a 1-quart/1-liter baking dish.

Heat the remaining butter in the saucepan with the milk and gently bring to a boil over medium heat.

Remove from the heat and stir in the breadcrumbs, 1 tablespoon of the superfine sugar, and the lemon rind.

Let stand and cool for 15 minutes, then beat in the egg yolks.

Pour the mixture into the baking dish, smooth the surface, and bake in the center of the oven for about 30 minutes, until it is set. Spread over the jelly.

Whisk the egg whites in the mixing bowl until very thick, then gradually add the remaining superfine sugar. Continue until all the sugar has been added.

Spoon the meringue over the dessert and make sure the meringue covers it completely. Swirl the meringue into attractive peaks and sprinkle with the granulated sugar.

Bake again in the center of the oven for 10–15 minutes until the meringue is golden brown but still soft. Serve warm.

Fruits

Apple & Blackberry Crumble

serves 4

2 lb/900 g cooking apples

10½ oz/300 g blackberries, fresh or frozen

heaping ¼ cup dark brown sugar

1 tsp ground cinnamon

custard or heavy cream, to serve

crumble topping

heaping ½ cup self-rising flour

¾ cup whole-wheat all-purpose flour

1 stick unsalted butter

heaping ¼ cup raw brown sugar

Preheat the oven to 400°F/200°C. Peel and core the apples, then cut into chunks. Put in a bowl with the blackberries, dark brown sugar, and cinnamon, and mix together, then transfer to an ovenproof baking dish.

To make the crumble, sift the self-rising flour into a bowl and stir in the whole-wheat flour. Rub in the butter with your fingertips until the mixture resembles coarse breadcrumbs. Stir in the raw brown sugar.

Spread the crumble over the apples and bake in the preheated oven for 40–45 minutes, or until the apples are soft and the crumble is golden brown and crisp. Serve with some custard on the side.

Fruit Cobbler

serves 6

2 lb/900 g fresh berries
and currants, such as
blackberries, blueberries,
raspberries, red currants,
and black currants

about ½ cup superfine
sugar

2 tbsp cornstarch

Cobbler topping

1⅓ cups all-purpose flour

2 tsp baking powder

pinch of salt

4 tbsp unsalted butter,
diced and chilled

2 tbsp superfine sugar

¾ cup buttermilk

1 tbsp raw brown sugar

light or heavy cream,
to serve

Preheat the oven to 400°F/200°C. Pick over the fruit, then mix with the superfine sugar and cornstarch and put in a 10-inch/25-cm shallow, ovenproof dish.

To make the topping, sift the flour, baking powder, and salt into a large bowl. Rub in the butter until the mixture resembles breadcrumbs, then stir in the superfine sugar. Pour in the buttermilk and mix to a soft dough.

Drop spoonfuls of the dough on top of the fruit roughly, so that it doesn't completely cover the fruit. Sprinkle with the raw brown sugar and bake in the preheated oven for 25–30 minutes, or until the crust is golden and the fruit is tender.

Remove from the oven and let stand for a few minutes before serving with cream.

Pears in Wine

serves 4

4 large pears

heaping 1 cup superfine sugar

1 cinnamon stick or vanilla bean

⅔ cup water

⅔ cup red wine

Peel the pears, leaving the stalks intact. Cut a thin slice off the bottom of each pear so that it will stand upright.

Put the sugar and cinnamon stick in a large saucepan, add the water, and bring to a boil over medium heat, stirring until the sugar has dissolved. Add the pears, reduce the heat, cover, and then simmer for 15 minutes.

Pour in the wine and simmer, uncovered, for an additional 15 minutes, or until the pears are just tender. Remove the pears with a slotted spoon and stand them in a serving dish.

Remove and discard the cinnamon stick and bring the wine syrup back to a boil. Boil rapidly until thickened, then pour the syrup over the pears and let cool. Chill for at least 1 hour before serving.

Flambéed Peaches

serves 4

3 tbsp unsalted butter

3 tbsp brown sugar

4 tbsp orange juice

4 peaches, peeled, halved, and pitted

2 tbsp amaretto or peach brandy

4 tbsp toasted slivered almonds

Heat the butter, brown sugar, and orange juice in a large, heavy-bottom skillet over low heat, stirring continuously, until the butter has melted and the sugar has dissolved.

Add the peaches and cook for 1–2 minutes on each side, or until golden.

Add the amaretto and ignite with a match or taper. When the flames have died down, transfer to serving dishes, sprinkle with toasted slivered almonds, and serve.

Banana Fritters

serves 4

½ cup all-purpose flour

2 tbsp rice flour

1 tbsp superfine sugar

1 egg, separated

⅔ cup coconut milk

sunflower oil for
deep-frying

4 large bananas

to serve

1 tsp confectioners' sugar

1 tsp ground cinnamon

lime wedges

Sift the all-purpose flour, rice flour, and sugar into a bowl and make a well in the center. Add the egg yolk and coconut milk. Beat the mixture until a smooth, thick batter forms.

Whisk the egg white in a clean, dry bowl until stiff enough to hold soft peaks. Fold it into the batter lightly and evenly.

Heat a 2½-inch/6-cm depth of oil in a large saucepan to 350–375°F/180–190°C, or until a cube of bread browns in 30 seconds. Cut the bananas in half crosswise, then dip them quickly into the batter to coat them.

Drop the bananas carefully into the hot oil and deep-fry in batches for 2–3 minutes, until golden brown, turning once.

Drain on paper towels. Sprinkle with confectioners' sugar and cinnamon and serve immediately, with lime wedges for squeezing juice as desired.

Broiled Cinnamon Oranges

serves 4

4 large oranges

1 tsp ground cinnamon

1 tbsp raw brown sugar

Preheat the broiler to high. Cut the oranges in half and discard any seeds. Using a sharp or curved grapefruit knife, carefully cut the flesh away from the skin by cutting around the edge of the fruit. Cut across the segments to loosen the flesh into bite-size pieces that will spoon out easily.

Place the orange halves, cut side up, in a shallow, heatproof dish. Mix the cinnamon with the sugar in a small bowl and sprinkle evenly over the orange halves. Cook under the preheated broiler for 3–5 minutes, or until the sugar has caramelized and is golden and bubbling. Serve at once.

Baked Apples

4 medium-size cooking apples

1 tbsp lemon juice

⅓ cup blueberries

⅓ cup raisins

3 tbsp chopped, toasted mixed nuts

½ tsp ground cinnamon

2 tbsp packed brown sugar

scant 1¼ cups red wine

2 tsp cornstarch

4 tsp water

heavy cream, to serve

Preheat the oven to 400°F/200°C. Using a sharp knife, score a line around the center of each apple. Core the apples, then brush the center with the lemon juice to prevent discoloration. Transfer them to a small roasting pan.

Place the blueberries and raisins in a bowl, then add the nuts, cinnamon, and sugar. Mix together well. Pile the mixture into the center of each apple, then pour over the wine.

Transfer the stuffed apples to the preheated oven and bake for 40–45 minutes, or until tender. Remove from the oven, then lift the apples out of the oven and keep them warm.

Blend the cornstarch with the water, then add the mixture to the cooking juices in the roasting pan. Transfer to the stove top and cook over medium heat, stirring, until thickened. Remove from the heat and pour over the apples. Serve the apples with the cream.

Fruit Crêpes

serves 4

crêpes

scant 1 cup all-purpose flour

pinch of salt

2 eggs

1¼ cups milk

2–3 tbsp vegetable oil

filling

1 banana

1 tbsp lemon juice

2 nectarines, pitted and cut into small pieces

1 mango, peeled, pitted, and cut into small pieces

3 kiwis, peeled and cut into small pieces

2 tbsp maple syrup

confectioners' sugar, to dust

whipped cream, to serve

To make the crêpes sift the flour and salt into a bowl. Whisk in the eggs and milk. Cover with plastic wrap and chill for 30 minutes.

To make the filling, peel and slice the banana and put into a large bowl. Pour over the lemon juice and stir gently until coated. Add the nectarines, mango, kiwis, and maple syrup, and stir together gently until mixed.

Heat a little oil in a skillet until hot. Remove the crêpe batter from the refrigerator and add a large spoonful to the skillet. Cook over high heat until golden, then turn over and cook briefly on the other side. Remove from the skillet and keep warm. Cook the other crêpes in the same way, stacking them on a plate. Keep warm. Divide the fruit filling among the crêpes and fold into triangles or roll into horns. Dust with confectioners' sugar and serve with whipped cream.

Pear Crêpes with Chocolate Sauce

serves 4

crêpes

scant 1 cup all-purpose flour

pinch of salt

3 eggs

generous 1 cup milk

2 tbsp lemon oil or vegetable oil

filling

9 oz/250 g pears

8 cloves

3 tbsp currants

pinch of ground allspice

sauce

4½ oz/125 g semisweet chocolate, broken into small pieces

2½ tbsp butter

6 tbsp water

Preheat the oven to 325°F/160°C.

To make the crêpes, sift the flour and salt into a bowl. Whisk in the eggs and milk to make a batter. Cover with plastic wrap and chill for 30 minutes. Heat a little oil in a skillet until hot. Add a large spoonful of the batter and cook over high heat until golden, then turn over and cook briefly on the other side. Cook the other crêpes in the same way, stacking them on a plate.

To make the filling, bring a saucepan of water to a boil. Peel and slice the pears; add to the pan with the cloves and currants. Reduce the heat and simmer for 5 minutes. Remove from the heat, drain, and discard the cloves. Let cool a little. Oil an ovenproof dish. Stir the allspice into the fruit; divide among the crêpes. Fold the crêpes into triangles. Arrange in the dish and bake for 15 minutes. To make the sauce, melt the chocolate and butter with the water in a small saucepan, stirring. Serve the crêpes with the sauce.

Broiled Honeyed Figs with Sabayon

serves 4

8 fresh figs, cut in half

4 tbsp honey

2 fresh rosemary sprigs, leaves removed and finely chopped (optional)

3 eggs

Preheat the broiler to high. Arrange the figs, cut side up, on the broiler pan. Brush with half the honey and sprinkle over the rosemary, if using.

Cook under the preheated broiler for 5–6 minutes, or until just starting to caramelize.

Meanwhile, to make the sabayon, in a large, heatproof bowl, lightly whisk the eggs with the remaining honey, then place over a saucepan of simmering water. Using an electric mixer, beat the eggs and honey together for 10 minutes, or until pale and thick.

Put 4 fig halves on each of 4 serving plates, add a generous spoonful of the sabayon, and serve at once.

Warm Currants in Cassis

serves 4

3 cups black currants

2 cups red currants

4 tbsp superfine sugar

grated rind and juice of
1 orange

2 tsp arrowroot

2 tbsp crème de cassis

whipped cream or yogurt,
to serve

Using a fork, strip the black currants and red currants from their stalks and put in a saucepan.

Add the superfine sugar and orange rind and juice and heat gently, stirring, until the sugar has dissolved. Bring to a boil and simmer gently for 5 minutes.

Strain the currants and place in a bowl, then return the juice to the pan.

Blend the arrowroot with a little water and mix into the juice in the pan. Boil the mixture until thickened.

Set aside to cool slightly, then stir in the crème de cassis.

Serve in individual dishes with whipped cream.

Raspberry Brûlées

serves 4

9 oz/250 g raspberries

1 tbsp lemon juice

2 tbsp raspberry preserve

½ cup mascarpone cheese

½ cup heavy cream, lightly whipped

1 tsp vanilla extract

6 tbsp superfine sugar

whole raspberries, to decorate

Put the raspberries and lemon juice into a saucepan and stir over low heat for about 5 minutes, until they start to soften. Remove from the heat, stir in the preserve, then divide among 4 ramekins.

Preheat the broiler to hot. In a bowl, mix together the mascarpone cheese, cream, and vanilla extract. Spoon the mixture over the raspberries and level the surfaces. Sprinkle the sugar over the top, allowing 1½ tablespoons per ramekin. Cook under the preheated broiler, as close to the flames or element as possible, for 2–3 minutes, until the sugar caramelizes. Remove from the broiler, decorate with whole raspberries, and serve immediately. Alternatively, to serve chilled, let cool to room temperature, then cover with plastic wrap and place in the refrigerator to chill for 3–4 hours.

Banana Splits

serves 4

4 bananas

vanilla ice cream

1¼ cups milk

1 tsp vanilla extract

3 egg yolks

½ cup superfine sugar

1¼ cups heavy cream, whipped

chocolate rum sauce

4½ oz/125 g semisweet chocolate, broken into small pieces

2½ tbsp butter

6 tbsp water

1 tbsp rum

6 tbsp chopped mixed nuts, to decorate

To make the ice cream, heat the milk and vanilla extract in a saucepan until almost boiling. In a bowl, beat together the egg yolks and sugar. Remove the milk from the heat and stir a little into the egg mixture. Transfer the mixture to the pan. Stir over low heat until thick. Do not boil. Remove from the heat. Let cool for 30 minutes, fold in the cream, cover with plastic wrap, and chill for 1 hour. Transfer to an ice-cream maker and process for 15 minutes. Alternatively, transfer to a freezerproof container and freeze for 1 hour, then place in a bowl and beat to break up the ice crystals. Return to in the container and freeze for 30 minutes. Repeat twice more, freezing for 30 minutes and whisking each time.

To make the sauce, melt the chocolate and butter with the water together in a saucepan, stirring. Remove from the heat and stir in the rum. Peel the bananas, slice them lengthwise, and arrange on 4 serving dishes. Top with ice cream and nuts and serve with the sauce.

Fresh Fruit Salad

serves 4

6 tbsp superfine sugar

1¾ cups water

½ tsp ground allspice

grated rind of ½ lemon

1 papaya

1 mango

1 pineapple

4 oranges, peeled and cut into segments

1 cup strawberries, hulled and quartered

light or heavy cream, to serve (optional)

Place the sugar, water, allspice, and lemon rind in a saucepan. Bring to a boil, stirring continuously, then continue to boil for 1 minute. Remove from the heat and let cool to room temperature. Transfer to a pitcher or bowl, cover with plastic wrap, and chill in the refrigerator for at least 1 hour.

Peel and halve the papaya and remove the seeds. Cut the flesh into small chunks or slices, and place in a large bowl. Cut the mango either side lengthwise, close to the pit. Remove and discard the pit. Peel and cut the flesh into small chunks or slices, and add to the bowl. Cut off the top and bottom of the pineapple and remove the hard skin. Cut the pineapple in half lengthwise, then into quarters, and remove the tough core. Cut the remaining flesh into small pieces and add to the bowl. Add the orange segments and strawberries. Pour over the chilled syrup, cover with plastic wrap, and chill until required.

Remove the fruit salad from the refrigerator and serve with the cream, if using.

Summer Fruit Mold

serves 6

2 lb/900 g mixed berries, such as raspberries and blackberries

¾ cup superfine sugar

½ cup milk

8 slices day-old white bread, crusts removed

Hull the berries and put them in a bowl. Sprinkle with the sugar and set aside.

Sprinkle the milk over the slices of bread to soften them slightly. Line the bottom and sides of an ovenproof bowl with two thirds of the bread, cutting it to fit but overlap the edges slightly. Spoon the berries into the bowl and place the remaining bread slices on top, cutting to fit and making sure that the fruit is completely covered.

Place a circle of wax paper on top of the last layer of bread. Put a plate or saucer, slightly smaller than the diameter of the bowl, on top, then place a weight, such as a heavy can of fruit, on the plate. Let chill in the refrigerator for at least 8 hours.

To serve, remove the weight, plate, and wax paper. Invert a serving dish on top of the bowl and, holding them together, reverse and shake sharply—the mold should slide out.

Upside-Down Tropical Fruit Mold

serves 8

¾ cup butter, softened, plus extra for greasing

scant 1 cup brown sugar

3 eggs

1¼ cups self-rising flour

1 tsp ground allspice

topping

4 tbsp butter, softened

¼ cup brown sugar

2 bananas

1 small pineapple

1 mango

Preheat the oven to 350°F/180°C. Grease a deep 8-inch/20-cm round cake pan.

To make the topping, spread the butter evenly over the bottom of the pan and sprinkle the sugar on top. Peel the bananas and slice thickly, then peel the pineapple and mango and cut into chunks. Mix the fruit together and pile evenly over the bottom of the pan.

To make the cake, place the butter, sugar, and eggs in a bowl and sift in the flour and allspice. Beat together until light and fluffy, then spread the batter over the fruit. Bake in the preheated oven for 50 minutes–1 hour, or until well risen and firm to the touch. Let stand in the pan for 10 minutes, then loosen the edges with a spatula and turn out onto a serving plate.

Pavlova

serves 4

6 egg whites

pinch of cream of tartar

pinch of salt

1⅓ cups superfine sugar

2½ cups heavy cream

1 tsp vanilla extract

2 kiwis, peeled and sliced

9 oz/250 g strawberries, hulled and sliced

3 ripe peaches, sliced

1 ripe mango, peeled and sliced

2 tbsp orange liqueur, such as Cointreau

fresh mint leaves, to decorate

Preheat the oven to 225°F/110°C. Line 3 baking sheets with parchment paper, then draw an 8½-inch/22-cm circle in the center of each one. Beat the egg whites into stiff peaks. Mix in the cream of tartar and salt. Gradually add 7 oz/ 200 g of the sugar. Beat for 2 minutes, until glossy. Fill a piping bag with the meringue mixture and pipe enough to fill each circle, doming them slightly in the center. Bake for 3 hours. Remove from the oven. Let cool.

Whip together the cream and vanilla extract with the remaining sugar. Put the fruit into a separate bowl and stir in the liqueur. Put one meringue circle onto a plate, then spread over one third of the sugared cream. Spread over one third of the fruit, then top with a meringue circle. Spread over another third of cream, then another third of fruit. Top with the last meringue circle. Spread over the remaining cream, followed by the rest of the fruit. Decorate with mint leaves and serve.

Chocolate-Dipped Fruit

serves 4

12 Cape gooseberries

7 squares semisweet chocolate, broken into pieces

1 tbsp corn oil

12 small strawberries

Line a baking sheet with parchment paper. Peel back the papery outer case from each Cape gooseberry and twist at the top to make a "handle."

Put the chocolate and oil in a small, heatproof bowl, then set the bowl over a saucepan of barely simmering water and heat until the chocolate has melted. Remove from the heat, then stir and let cool until tepid.

Dip the fruit in the chocolate mixture and let any excess drain back into the bowl. The fruit does not need to be completely coated.

Set the fruit on the prepared baking sheet. If the chocolate forms a "foot" on the paper, it is too warm, so let cool slightly. If the chocolate in the bowl begins to set, warm it gently over the pan of simmering water. Chill the dipped fruit in the refrigerator for 30 minutes, or until the chocolate is set, then peel away from the paper. Serve on their own, or use to decorate another dessert.

Chilled Desserts

Tiramisu

serves 4

scant 1 cup strong black coffee, cooled to room temperature

4 tbsp orange liqueur, such as Cointreau

3 tbsp orange juice

16 Italian sponge fingers

1 cup mascarpone cheese

1¼ cups heavy cream, lightly whipped

3 tbsp confectioners' sugar

grated rind of 1 orange

2¼ oz/60 g chocolate, grated

to decorate

chopped toasted almonds

crystallized orange peel

chocolate shavings

Pour the cooled coffee into a pitcher and stir in the orange liqueur and orange juice. Put 8 of the sponge fingers in the bottom of a serving dish, then pour over half of the coffee mixture.

Place the mascarpone cheese in a separate bowl along with the cream, confectioners' sugar, and orange rind and mix well together. Spread half of the mascarpone cheese mixture over the coffee-soaked sponge fingers, then arrange the remaining sponge fingers on top. Pour over the remaining coffee mixture and then spread over the remaining mascarpone cheese mixture. Scatter over the grated chocolate and chill in the refrigerator for at least 2 hours. Serve decorated with chopped toasted almonds, crystallized orange peel, and chocolate shavings.

Rich Chocolate Roulade

serves 4–6

butter, for greasing

6 oz/175 g semisweet chocolate, chopped

3 tbsp warm water

2 tbsp coffee-flavored liqueur, such as Kahlúa or Tia Maria (optional)

5 eggs, separated

scant 1 cup superfine sugar

filling

2 cups heavy cream

1/3 cup confectioners' sugar, sifted, plus extra for dusting

3 tbsp unsweetened cocoa

2 tsp espresso coffee powder, dissolved in 1 tbsp boiling water

halved strawberries, to decorate

Preheat the oven to 350°F/180°C. Grease and line a 14 x 10-inch/35 x 25-cm jelly roll pan.

Put the chocolate into a heatproof bowl and set over a saucepan of simmering water, stirring occasionally, until melted. Stir in the water and the liqueur, if using. Whisk the egg yolks and superfine sugar in a bowl until pale. Beat the chocolate into the yolks. Whisk the egg whites in a bowl until stiff, then fold into the chocolate. Pour into the pan and bake for 15 minutes. Remove, cover with wax paper, and let cool for 3–4 hours. Meanwhile, whisk the filling ingredients together in a bowl until thick. Cover with plastic wrap and chill.

Turn the cake out onto wax paper dusted with confectioners' sugar. Discard the lining paper. Reserve 4 tablespoons of the filling, then spread the rest over the cake, leaving a 1-inch/2.5-cm border. Starting from a short side, roll up the cake. Discard the paper. Pipe the remaining filling on top, decorate with strawberries, and serve.

Chocolate Cheesecake

serves 4–6

base

4 tbsp butter, melted, plus extra for greasing

scant 1½ cups graham crackers, finely crushed

2 tsp unsweetened cocoa

halved kumquats, to decorate

chocolate layer

3¾ cups, mascarpone cheese

1¾ cups confectioners' sugar, sifted

juice of ½ orange

finely grated rind of 1 orange

6 oz/175 g semisweet chocolate, melted

2 tbsp brandy

chocolate leaves

12–16 firm, fresh, smooth nontoxic leaves, such as bay or citrus

6 oz/175 g semisweet chocolate, melted

Grease an 8-inch/20-cm loose-bottom cake pan.

To make the base, place the crushed crackers, cocoa, and melted butter in a large bowl and mix well. Press the cracker mixture evenly over the bottom of the prepared pan.

For the chocolate layer, place the mascarpone cheese and confectioners' sugar in a bowl and stir in the orange juice and rind. Add the melted chocolate and brandy, and mix together until thoroughly combined. Spread the chocolate mixture evenly over the cracker layer. Cover with plastic wrap and chill for at least 4 hours.

To make the chocolate leaves, wipe the leaves gently with paper towels. Using a pastry brush or clean paintbrush, carefully coat one side of each leaf with the melted chocolate, working from the center to the edges. Do not let the chocolate run over the edges or onto the other side of the leaves, because it will make them almost impossible to remove without breaking the decoration. Place the leaves, coated side up, on a sheet of wax paper to set. When the chocolate has set, carefully peel away the leaves from the stalk ends, handling the chocolate leaves as little as possible.

Remove the cheesecake from the refrigerator, turn out onto a serving platter, and decorate with the chocolate leaves and kumquat halves. Serve immediately.

Trifle

serves 4

fruit layer

12 ladyfingers

2 tbsp strawberry jelly

6 large strawberries, hulled and sliced

2 bananas, peeled and sliced

14 oz/400 g canned sliced peaches, drained

6 tbsp sherry

vanilla cream layer

scant 1¼ cups heavy cream

1 tsp vanilla extract

3 egg yolks

4 tbsp superfine sugar

topping

1¼ cups heavy cream

2 tbsp superfine sugar

chopped mixed nuts, toasted, to decorate

To make the fruit layer, spread the ladyfingers with jam, cut into bite-size pieces, and arrange in the bottom of a glass serving bowl. Scatter over the fruit, pour over the sherry, and set aside.

To make the vanilla cream, place the cream and vanilla extract in a saucepan and bring almost to a boil over low heat. Meanwhile, place the egg yolks and sugar in a baking dish and whisk together. Remove the cream mixture from the heat and gradually stir into the egg mixture. Return the mixture to the pan and warm over low heat, stirring, until thickened. Remove the custard from the heat and let cool for 30 minutes, then pour it over the fruit layer. Cover with plastic wrap and chill for 2½ hours.

Remove the trifle from the refrigerator. To make the topping, whip the cream and sugar together, then spread it evenly over the vanilla cream layer. Scatter the toasted, chopped mixed nuts over the top, then cover again with plastic wrap and chill for another 1½ hours. Serve chilled.

Crème Caramel

serves 4–6

butter, for greasing

1 cup superfine sugar

4 tbsp water

½ lemon

2 cups milk

1 vanilla bean

2 large eggs

2 large egg yolks

sugared fruit and fresh
mint leaves, to decorate

Preheat the oven to 325°F/160°C. Lightly grease the base and sides of two 1-pint/600-ml soufflé dishes. To make the caramel, place 2¾ oz/75 g sugar with the water in a saucepan over medium–high heat and cook, stirring, until the sugar dissolves. Boil until the syrup turns a deep golden brown. Immediately remove from the heat and squeeze in a few drops of lemon juice. Divide evenly between the soufflé dishes and swirl around. Set aside.

Pour the milk into a saucepan. Slit the vanilla pod lengthwise and add it to the milk. Bring to a boil, remove the saucepan from the heat and stir in the remaining sugar, stirring until it dissolves. Reserve.

Beat the eggs and egg yolks together in a bowl. Pour the milk mixture over them, whisking. Remove the vanilla pod. Strain the egg mixture into a bowl, then transfer and divide evenly between the soufflé dishes.

Place the dishes in a roasting pan with enough boiling water to come two thirds up the sides.

Bake in the preheated oven for 1–1¼ hours, or until a knife inserted in the center comes out clean. Leave to cool completely. Cover with plastic wrap and leave to chill for at least 24 hours.

Run a round-bladed knife around the edges of each dish. Place an up-turned serving plate with a rim on top, then invert the plate and dish, giving a sharp shake halfway over. Lift off the soufflé dishes and serve, decorated with fresh mint leaves.

Raspberries & Meringue Cream

serves 4

1 lb/500 g raspberries

4 tbsp amaretto or crème de framboise liqueur

1¼ cups heavy cream

6 small white meringues, coarsely crushed

Hull the raspberries, put them in a bowl, and sprinkle the liqueur over them. Cover with plastic wrap and let chill in the refrigerator for 2 hours.

Whisk the cream in a large bowl until soft peaks form, then fold the raspberries, with their juices, into it. Sprinkle the crushed meringues on top and gently fold in. Spoon into a serving dish and serve immediately.

Blueberry Gelatin with Cassis

serves 4–6

1 lb/450 g fresh blueberries, plus extra to decorate

⅔ cup water

scant 1¼ cups superfine sugar

¾ cup crème de cassis

2 envelopes granulated gelatin

3 tbsp water

fresh mint leaves, to decorate

confectioners' sugar, sifted, for dusting

Put the blueberries, water, and sugar in a saucepan and cook over medium heat until softened.

Remove from the heat and let cool. Crush the berries with a wooden spoon to make a smooth puree.

Pour the puree into a measuring cup and add the cassis. Make up to 20 fl oz/600 ml, adding extra water if necessary. Put the gelatin and the water in a heatproof cup and soak for 1–2 minutes, or until it is spongy. Put the cup in a small saucepan with enough water to come halfway up the sides, and heat over low heat for 2–3 minutes, or until the gelatin has dissolved and the mixture is clear.

Let cool until it is the same temperature as the fruit puree. Mix the blueberry mixture and the gelatin together and pour into individual serving glasses or into a jelly mold or a glass serving bowl. Cover with plastic wrap and chill in the refrigerator until set. Decorate with fresh blueberries and mint leaves, then dust with sifted confectioners' sugar and serve.

Cassata Semifreddo

serves 6–8

1 cup granulated sugar

⅔ cup water

2 egg whites

⅓ cup chopped blanched almonds

⅓ cup mixed dried fruit

⅓ cup candied cherries, chopped

1¼ cups whipping cream

Line a 9 x 5 x 3-inch/23 x 13 x 8-cm loaf pan or 1-quart/1.4-liter oblong freezerproof plastic container with wax paper, allowing it to hang over the edges of the container so that the ice cream can be easily removed. Put the sugar and water in a small heavy-bottom saucepan and heat gently, stirring, until the sugar has dissolved. Bring to a boil, then boil, without stirring, for 5 minutes, or until a syrup has formed. Do not allow it to brown.

Meanwhile, whisk the egg whites until stiff and dry. Drizzle the hot syrup in a thin stream onto the whisked egg whites, whisking all the time, until the mixture is thick, creamy, and fluffy. Continue whisking until the mixture is cold.

Add the nuts, dried fruit, and cherries to the meringue mixture and fold in until well blended. Whip the cream until it holds its shape, then fold in until well blended. Pour the mixture into the prepared pan, cover, and freeze for 5 hours, or until firm or required.

To serve the ice cream, uncover, stand the pan in hot water for a few seconds to loosen it, then invert it onto a serving dish. Remove the wax paper and, using a hot knife, cut into slices.

Tortoni

serves 6

4½ oz/125 g amaretti
cookies

1¼ cups heavy cream

⅔ cup light cream

1 cup confectioners' sugar

4 tbsp Marsala

Line an 8 x 4 x 2-inch/20 x 10 x 5-cm loaf pan or a 3½-cup oblong freezerproof plastic container with wax paper, allowing it to hang over the edges of the container so that the ice cream can be easily removed. Put the cookies in a food processor and process to form fine crumbs. Alternatively, put the cookies in a strong plastic bag and crush with a rolling pin.

Pour the heavy cream and light cream into a large bowl and whip together until the mixture holds its shape. Sift the confectioners' sugar into the whipped cream, then fold in with the Marsala. Fold in the cookies, reserving a third.

Pour the mixture into the prepared pan, smooth the surface and freeze, uncovered, for 5 hours, or until firm or required. Cover the container with a lid for storing.

Take the ice cream out of the freezer about 30 minutes before you are ready to serve it. Uncover, turn out onto a serving dish, and remove the wax paper. Let stand at room temperature to soften. Using a palette knife, press the reserved crushed cookies lightly onto the top and sides of the ice cream until it is evenly coated. Serve cut into thick slices.

Chocolate Mousses

serves 4

10½ oz/300 g semisweet chocolate

1½ tbsp unsalted butter

1 tbsp brandy

4 eggs, separated

unsweetened cocoa, for dusting

Break the chocolate into small pieces and place in a heatproof bowl set over a saucepan of simmering water. Add the butter and melt with the chocolate, stirring, until smooth. Remove from the heat, stir in the brandy, and let cool slightly. Add the egg yolks and beat until smooth.

In a separate bowl, whisk the egg whites until stiff peaks form, then fold them into the chocolate mixture. Put 4 stainless steel cooking rings on 4 small serving plates, then spoon the mixture into the rings and level the surfaces. Transfer to the refrigerator and chill for at least 4 hours, until set.

Take the mousses out of the refrigerator and remove the cooking rings. Dust with cocoa and serve.

Mascarpone Creams

serves 4

1⅓ cups amaretti cookies,
crushed

4 tbsp amaretto or
Maraschino

4 eggs, separated

heaping ¼ cup superfine
sugar

1 cup mascarpone cheese

toasted slivered almonds,
to decorate

Place the amaretti crumbs in a bowl, add the amaretto or Maraschino, and set aside to soak.

Meanwhile, beat the egg yolks with the sugar until pale and thick. Fold in the mascarpone cheese and soaked cookie crumbs.

Whisk the egg whites in a separate, spotlessly clean bowl until stiff, then gently fold into the cheese mixture. Divide the mascarpone cream among serving dishes and let chill for 1–2 hours. Sprinkle with toasted slivered almonds just before serving.

Apricot & Yogurt Cups

serves 4–6

2½ cups plain yogurt

few drops of almond extract

2–3 tsp honey, warmed

scant ½ cup whole blanched almonds

1 cup plumped dried apricots

Line a 12-cup muffin pan with small paper cake liners. Spoon the yogurt into a mixing bowl, add the almond extract and honey, and stir well. Using a small, sharp knife, cut the almonds into very thin slices and stir into the yogurt mixture. Using a pair of kitchen scissors, cut the apricots into small pieces, then stir into the yogurt.

Spoon the mixture into the paper liners and freeze for 1½–2 hours, or until just frozen. Serve at once.

Blueberry Cream Pots

serves 4

1 heaping tbsp custard powder

1¼ cups milk

2 tbsp superfine sugar

scant ¾ cup fresh or frozen blueberries, thawed if frozen

⅞ cup mascarpone cheese

Blend the custard powder with ¼ cup of the milk in a heatproof bowl. Bring the remaining milk to a boil in a small saucepan and pour over the custard mixture, mixing well. Return the custard to the pan and return to a boil over medium–low heat, stirring continuously, until thickened. Pour the custard into the bowl and sprinkle the sugar over the top of the custard to prevent a skin from forming. Cover and let cool completely.

Set aside 12 blueberries for decoration. Put the remaining blueberries and cold custard into a blender and process until smooth.

Spoon the mascarpone cheese and the blueberry mixture in alternate layers into 4 tall glasses. Decorate with the reserved blueberries and serve at once.

Layered Nectarine Creams

serves 4

4 nectarines, peeled, pitted, and sliced

2 tbsp amaretto liqueur

¾ cup curd cheese

1¼ cups peach-flavored yogurt

Set aside a few nectarine slices for decoration. Put the remainder in a bowl, add the liqueur, and toss gently, then set aside.

Beat the cheese and yogurt together in another bowl until thoroughly combined. Spoon half the mixture into 4 tall glasses. Divide the nectarine-and-liqueur mixture among them and top with the remaining cheese and yogurt mixture.

Decorate with the reserved nectarine slices and let chill in the refrigerator for at least 30 minutes before serving.

Rich Vanilla Ice Cream

serves 4–6

1¼ cups light cream

1¼ cups heavy cream

1 vanilla bean

4 large egg yolks

heaping ½ cup superfine sugar

Pour the light cream and the heavy cream into a large heavy-bottom saucepan. Split open the vanilla bean and scrape out the seeds into the cream, then add the whole vanilla bean, too. Bring almost to a boil, then remove from the heat and let infuse for 30 minutes.

Put the egg yolks and sugar in a large bowl and whisk together until pale and the mixture leaves a trail when the whisk is lifted. Remove the vanilla bean from the cream, then slowly add the cream to the egg mixture, stirring all the time with a wooden spoon. Strain the mixture into the rinsed-out pan or a double boiler and cook over low heat for 10–15 minutes, stirring all the time, until the mixture thickens enough to coat the back of the spoon. Do not let the mixture boil or it will curdle. Remove from the heat and let cool for at least 1 hour, stirring from time to time to prevent a skin from forming.

If using an ice-cream machine, churn the cold custard in the machine, following the manufacturer's instructions. Alternatively, freeze the custard in a freezerproof container, uncovered, for 1–2 hours, or until it starts to set around the edges. Turn the custard into a bowl and stir with a fork or beat in a food processor until smooth. Return to the freezer and freeze for an additional 2–3 hours, or until firm or required. Cover the container with a lid for storing.

Dark & White Chocolate Ice Cream

serves 4

6 egg yolks

scant ½ cup superfine sugar

1½ cups milk

¾ cup heavy cream

3½ oz/100 g semisweet chocolate

2¾ oz/75 g white chocolate, grated or finely chopped

fresh mint leaves, to decorate

Place the egg yolks and sugar in a heatproof bowl and beat until fluffy. Heat the milk, cream, and semisweet chocolate in a saucepan over low heat, stirring, until melted and almost boiling. Remove from the heat and whisk into the egg mixture. Return the mixture to the pan and cook, stirring, over low heat until thick. Do not let it simmer. Transfer to a heatproof bowl and cool. Cover with plastic wrap and chill for 1½ hours. Remove from the refrigerator and stir in the white chocolate.

Transfer to a freezerproof container and freeze for 1 hour. Remove from the freezer, transfer to a bowl and whisk to break up the ice crystals. Return to the container and freeze for 30 minutes. Repeat twice more, freezing for 30 minutes and whisking each time. Alternatively, transfer the mixture to an ice-cream machine and process for 15 minutes.

Scoop the ice cream into serving bowls, decorate with mint leaves, and serve.

Mango Sorbet

serves 4–6

2 large ripe mangoes

juice of 1 lemon

pinch of salt

heaping 1/2 cup sugar

3 tbsp water

Using a sharp knife, thinly peel the mangoes, holding them over a bowl to catch the juices. Cut the flesh away from the central pit and put in a food processor or blender. Add the mango juice, lemon juice, and salt and process to form a smooth puree. Push the mango puree through a nylon strainer into the bowl.

Put the sugar and water in a heavy-bottom saucepan and heat gently, stirring, until the sugar has dissolved. Bring to a boil, without stirring, then remove from the heat and let cool slightly.

Pour the syrup into the mango puree and mix well together. Let cool, then chill the mango syrup in the refrigerator for 2 hours, or until cold.

If using an ice-cream machine, churn the mixture in the machine, following the manufacturer's instructions. Alternatively, freeze the mixture in a freezerproof container, uncovered, for 3–4 hours, or until mushy. Turn the mixture into a bowl and stir with a fork or beat in a food processor to break down the ice crystals. Return to the freezer and freeze for an additional 3–4 hours, or until firm or required. Cover the container with a lid for storing.

Citrus Granita

serves 6

2 cups water

6 oranges

1½ lemons

¾ cup sugar

6 amaretti cookies,
to serve

Pare the rind from the fruit, then cut off and discard the pith. Slice a few thin strips of rind and put them to one side, separately from the large pieces. Squeeze the juice from the fruit.

Boil the sugar and water in a heavy-bottom saucepan and stir until the sugar dissolves. Boil, without stirring, for 10 minutes, until syrupy. Remove from the heat, stir in the large rind pieces, cover, and let cool.

Strain the cooled syrup into a freezerproof container and stir in the juice. Freeze, uncovered, for 4 hours, until slushy.

Blanch the thin rind strips in a saucepan of boiling water for 2 minutes. Drain and refresh with cold water. Pat dry with paper towels.

Remove the granita from the freezer and break up with a fork. Freeze again for an additional 4 hours, until hard.

Remove the granita from the freezer and let stand until slightly softened. Beat with a fork, then spoon into glasses and decorate with the rind strips. Serve with the cookies.